Contents

Would you rather: A (
hypothetical questions............................2

About the Author...................................4

Introduction...5

Helpful Guide.......................................7

Let's get drawing...................................8

More to Come....................................108

Other Books......................................109

WOULD YOU RATHER DOODLE: A collection of hilarious hypothetical questions
Vol:1

- By Clint Hammerstrike

To my awesome Brother in-law Chris thanks for the inspiration for this volume and all your encouragement! I would rather have you as my brother in-law than Donald Trump OR Kim Jung-Un any day!

About the Author

Someone with plenty of free time to write this book and enough imagination to create the name Clint Hammerstrike – seriously why wouldn't you!

What else is there to say other than you will be pleased to know this isn't my day job!

Introduction

Writing this book has been one of the most enjoyable things that I have ever done (I live a very dull life – queue sad music)! This is because I take great joy in pondering random scenarios and questions. If I built muscles every time I contemplated the questions would I rather X OR Y, I would be stronger than Thor (but I would rather be Wolverine).

I wrote this book to share with you some of the great conundrums we face in the modern age such as:

- Whether to go zorbing with a porcupine OR a skunk?
- Kiss a jellyfish OR a scorpion?
- Greet people by rubbing noses OR bottoms?

The great thing about this edition is that you not only get to ponder the complexity and bask in the pure joy of each hypothetical but you get to answer by drawing your favored choice!

This Doodle Edition could have you drawing anything from a Zombie Koala (see cover for inspiration) to you standing atop Mount Everest!

Remember all of these scenarios are for hypothetical entertainment and drawing purposes and should not be taken as a recommendation or an endorsement. You should never bathe with an alligator, lick an armpit or be Donald Trump. Did I really need to say that last one!?!

Helpful Guide

To aid you on this journey of self-discovery I have suggested a couple of rules to help you through.

Rule 1: You must answer. Even if you would rather do neither you MUST pick!

Rule 2: Don't rush your answer. Give yourself time to consider the sheer complexity and horror/joy of the choice!

Rule 3: Respect the opinion of those reading with you? Even when they are plainly wrong!

Rule 4: Take this seriously, we are considering the meaning of life do not even consider laughing!

Rule 5: Forget rule 4. Laugh, come on its dancing with King Kong OR Godzilla!

Rule 6: Draw whatever it is that you have chosen as your favoured option. How you decide to do this is up to you. Be as creative and detailed as you want. Send your best picture to clinthammerstrike@gmail.com and you could feature in a future edition! Alternatively share it online at: facebook.com/ClintHammerstrike

Let's get drawing

WOULD YOU RATHER:

Fart party poppers OR burp confetti?

WOULD YOU RATHER:

Eat a tablespoon of extra extra hot sauce OR get a brain freeze chugging a slush puppy?

WOULD YOU RATHER:

Not give up your seat on a train to a pensioner OR a pregnant woman?

WOULD YOU RATHER:

Have a hairy nose OR hairy ears?

WOULD YOU RATHER:

Brush your teeth with a squirrel OR a teacup pig?

WOULD YOU RATHER:

Suck on a hiker's socks OR lick a sumo wrestler's nappy?

WOULD YOU RATHER:

Eat someone else's scab OR earwax?

WOULD YOU RATHER:

Rub hot sauce OR vinegar into your eye?

WOULD YOU RATHER:

Be able to make people dance OR sing by shaking their hand?

WOULD YOU RATHER:

Be Superman OR Ironman?

WOULD YOU RATHER:

Go zorbing with a porcupine OR a skunk?

WOULD YOU RATHER:

Be trapped in a lift with a couple kissing OR fighting?

WOULD YOU RATHER:

Climb to the top of Mount Everest OR be Knighted?

WOULD YOU RATHER:

Live in a penthouse suite OR a country cottage?

WOULD YOU RATHER:

Always be sweaty OR itchy?

WOULD YOU RATHER:

Have the trunk of an elephant OR the legs of a giraffe?

WOULD YOU RATHER:

Have a finger for a tongue OR tongues for fingers?

WOULD YOU RATHER:

Eat a rat OR wear it as a necklace?

WOULD YOU RATHER:

Eat a monkey that tastes of cheese OR a llama that tastes of bacon?

WOULD YOU RATHER:

Be the strongest OR the smartest person in the world?

WOULD YOU RATHER:

Juggle lobsters OR hedgehogs?

WOULD YOU RATHER:

Sleep in a bed with spiders OR cockroaches?

WOULD YOU RATHER:

Have a house with 101 cats OR dogs?

WOULD YOU RATHER:

Be a lion tamer OR a trapeze artist?

WOULD YOU RATHER:

Sweat gravy OR custard?

WOULD YOU RATHER:

Have a nose twice as small OR twice as big as normal?

WOULD YOU RATHER:

Your skin has the pattern of a zebra OR a leopard?

WOULD YOU RATHER:

Be able to swim like a dolphin OR climb like a monkey?

WOULD YOU RATHER:

Be lost in the desert OR in the jungle?

WOULD YOU RATHER:

Be able to fly OR be super strong?

WOULD YOU RATHER:

Be Donald Trump OR a human cannon ball?

WOULD YOU RATHER:

Kiss a jellyfish OR a scorpion?

WOULD YOU RATHER:

Dance with King Kong OR Godzilla?

WOULD YOU RATHER:

Be the tallest person in the world OR the shortest?

WOULD YOU RATHER:

Have feet as long as your legs OR legs as long as your feet?

WOULD YOU RATHER:

Be covered in feathers OR fur?

WOULD YOU RATHER:

Lick the back of a stranger knees OR their armpits?

WOULD YOU RATHER:

Live at the South Pole OR North Pole?

WOULD YOU RATHER:

Go back one hundred years into the past OR forward one hundred years into the future?

WOULD YOU RATHER:

Shower in tea OR coffee?

WOULD YOU RATHER:

Have a dog with a parrot face OR a shark face?

WOULD YOU RATHER:

Greet people by rubbing noses OR bottoms together?

WOULD YOU RATHER:

Go paintballing in a mankini/bikini OR a hospital gown?

WOULD YOU RATHER:

Eat a deep fried Mars Bar OR a doughnut burger?

WOULD YOU RATHER:

Re-take your High School exams OR have major dental work?

WOULD YOU RATHER:

Have the face of a Panda OR a lion?

WOULD YOU RATHER:

Cook dinner for the Queen of England OR the President of the USA?

WOULD YOU RATHER:

Tightrope walk across the Grand Canyon holding a snake OR a scorpion?

WOULD YOU RATHER:

Spend the day with a crab OR a Gecko in your underwear?

WOULD YOU RATHER:

Run a marathon carrying a fridge OR without any trainers?

WOULD YOU RATHER:

Have an office job OR work outside?

WOULD YOU RATHER:

Be a tree OR a flower?

WOULD YOU RATHER:

Spend a day in the life of a movie star OR Rock/Pop star?

WOULD YOU RATHER:

Get married and discover you partner was an assassin OR has a secret family?

WOULD YOU RATHER:

Be a skilled archer OR sword fighter?

WOULD YOU RATHER:

Be a Samurai or a Medieval Knight?

WOULD YOU RATHER:

Never be able to use a knife OR a fork again?

WOULD YOU RATHER:

Have to drink out of your shoe OR a stranger's motorcycle helmet?

WOULD YOU RATHER:

Have a lightsabre OR a hover board (one that actually hovers not a rubbish one with wheels)?

WOULD YOU RATHER:

Be a contestant in "The Hunger Games" OR be a gladiator in ancient Rome?

WOULD YOU RATHER:

Be pursued by Zombie Koalas OR Wereblobfishes (werewolf + blob fish hybrid)?

WOULD YOU RATHER:

Have to wear a sombrero OR a Hawaiian shirt for the rest of your life?

WOULD YOU RATHER:

Have a bird's nest OR a squirrel's drey (nest) in your hair?

WOULD YOU RATHER:

Be an airplane pilot OR a boat captain?

WOULD YOU RATHER:

Drink 10 pints of your own urine OR 1 pint of someone else's?

WOULD YOU RATHER:

Be able to do a handstand OR a cartwheel?

WOULD YOU RATHER:

Eat cabbage OR cauliflower for every meal (including breakfast) for the rest of your life?

WOULD YOU RATHER:

Have a colonic irrigation OR give someone else one?

WOULD YOU RATHER:

Be a sloth OR a tiger?

WOULD YOU RATHER:

Poo OR vomit every time someone says your name?

WOULD YOU RATHER:

Be able to turn invisible OR move things with your mind?

WOULD YOU RATHER:

Eat a tub or butter OR a 6 pack of eggs raw?

WOULD YOU RATHER:

Be punched by a gorilla OR kicked by a kangaroo?

WOULD YOU RATHER:

Wear a leotard OR a wedding dress for the rest of your life?

WOULD YOU RATHER:

Wear clown make up or goth make up for the rest of your life?

WOULD YOU RATHER:

Hit the game winning home run OR throw the game winning pitch?

WOULD YOU RATHER:

Be a mermaid/man OR a unicorn?

WOULD YOU RATHER:

Be a cat OR a dog?

WOULD YOU RATHER:

Be able to juggle OR ride a unicycle?

WOULD YOU RATHER:

Have a tattoo of a lobster wearing a tuxedo OR a tortoise playing a banjo?

WOULD YOU RATHER:

Be an artist or an author?

WOULD YOU RATHER:

Be raised by lions OR monkeys?

WOULD YOU RATHER:

Always have smelly fish OR smelly cheese in your pocket?

WOULD YOU RATHER:

Have a third arm growing out of your head OR your stomach?

WOULD YOU RATHER:

Be able to transform into a penguin OR a meerkat?

WOULD YOU RATHER:

Fight 1 brown bear OR 30 Lemurs?

WOULD YOU RATHER:

Be a chef OR a florist?

WOULD YOU RATHER:

Have a unicorn horn or a halo on your head?

WOULD YOU RATHER:

Lick a shower floor OR the gap in-between someone's toes?

WOULD YOU RATHER:

Take a bath with an alligator OR a shark?

WOULD YOU RATHER:

Be a contortionist OR a magician?

WOULD YOU RATHER:

Every time you sneeze a parrot OR a puppy comes out?

WOULD YOU RATHER:

Be able to poop out burgers OR pizza?

WOULD YOU RATHER:

Have chocolate bars for fingers OR crème eggs for eyes?

WOULD YOU RATHER:

Live in a house made of chocolate OR cake?

WOULD YOU RATHER:

Wear a toga OR a Pokémon onesie to a job interview?

WOULD YOU RATHER:

Be a detective OR a doctor?

WOULD YOU RATHER:

Skydive OR bungee jump?

WOULD YOU RATHER:

Be trapped in space for a year on your own OR with a person you hate?

WOULD YOU RATHER:

Eat your bodyweight in earwax or Bogeys?

More to Come

Congratulations you have made your way through the weird and wonderful world of hypothetical questions.

I hope that you have enjoyed yourself along the way and managed to create the new Mona Lisa – or perhaps just a stick person vomiting when their name is called. Is there much difference between the two?

If you have enjoyed this book or feel like you still need further hypothetical therapy, please check out the other titles in this series available in e-book and paperback on Amazon.

Also if you are feeling brave please send me through your best picture and it could feature in the next doodle edition. Please send any picture to: **clinthammerstrike@gmail.com** or share it online at: **facebook.com/ClintHammerstrike**

More hypothetical fun can be found on: Facebook at:
https://www.facebook.com/ClintHammerstrike
or **www.clinthammerstrike.com**
or **@Hammerstrikewyr**

Other Books

If you have enjoyed this book, please check out these other titles in the series:

> Would You Rather Random: A Collection of Hypothetical Question by Clint Hammerstrike. – Containing over 300 original "would you rather" questions and unique scenarios. Available in paperback and e-book.

Printed in Poland
by Amazon Fulfillment
Poland Sp. z o.o., Wrocław